REDSTONE

-v-

KELLY

YOMI MAKANJUOLA

REDSTONE-v-KELLY

Cover design by CreateSpace

Manufactured in the UK by CreateSpace

*Order paperback and e-Book versions at
www.amazon.com*

To all the *Trampled Victims*

of the *Great Recession*

CHAPTER 1

Warren Buffett, arguably the most influential investor in living memory, famously warned in his 2002 letter to his company's shareholders: "*…derivatives are financial weapons of mass destruction, carrying dangers that, while now latent, are potentially lethal. We view them as time bombs, both for the parties that deal in them and the economic system.*"

Before your eyes glaze over, or you otherwise let rip an involuntary yawn, rest assured that this story is not a technical yarn but rather the tale of two young men who got ensnared in the slipstream of the worst economic crisis since the *Great Depression*. This still begs the question of why the author has chosen to 'immortalise' two minor protagonists in the most consequential financial meltdown in nearly a century. Could it be because the mass media seldom feature such stories?

To mollify readers who might squabble over Mr. Buffett's vocabulary, *derivatives* are complex financial contracts that cynics could rightly argue were designed by insiders to be deliberately impenetrable. Confounding even technocrats tasked as financial regulators, newspaper headlines in the wake of the 2008 crash introduced the public to cryptic terms such as mortgage derivatives, collaterised debt obligations (CDO), and credit default swaps (CDS). For the benefit of the everyday citizen, the basic knowledge of the home mortgage as an investment vehicle provides a narrow insight into the financial markets which trade stocks, bonds, and all manner of exotic financial instruments.

Essentially, what the clever operatives on Wall Street, the City of London, and other global financial centres did, prior to the 2008 housing crisis, was to bundle or consolidate masses of *sub-prime mortgage* investments and trade them in tranches across the global financial system. Aided and abetted by credit rating agencies, they sought to promote market liquidity in order to facilitate easy credit to borrowers. The time bomb that Warren Buffett cited in his letter alluded to arcane derivatives, including mainly *sub-prime mortgage* contracts, which built up into a bubble that eventually burst, and then triggered a devastating credit crunch.

With the benefit of hindsight, the prefix "sub", as in *sub-prime mortgage*, was a clear red flag. Words such as sub-par or sub-standard connote inferiority, and ordinarily should make anyone wary. As such, a *sub-prime mortgage* was indicative of a less than 'prime' or conventional mortgage. Defined as a category of mortgage issued by lending institutions to borrowers with low credit ratings, its share of the housing market steadily grew to dangerous levels, particularly in the US.

To add some perspective, the *sub-prime mortgage* crisis of the late 2000s had its origin in a deregulatory environment dating from the 1990s, which aimed to boost home ownership across social classes, including among low-income earners. Ominously, this laudable goal would expose high-leverage borrowers to loan defaults during the ensuing economic downturn. Two decades earlier in the UK, the conservative government of Prime Minister Margaret Thatcher had introduced a bill in parliament that encouraged Britons to buy their council houses, as a pillar of her government's free-market economic philosophy.

Subsequently, accelerating deregulation of financial markets relaxed official controls and freed up institutions to operate across a wider range of territories and activities. This meant that mortgages that existed only in the domain of the traditional banking system could now be traded as over-the-counter transactions in open markets, within and outside the US, with minimal regulatory oversight. By effectively liberalising credit, and making it easier to borrow money, this resulted in a huge increase in personal indebtedness, including mortgage debt. During the Tony Blair years, private home ownership experienced a boom in the UK, though on a relatively smaller scale than in the US.

By sheer coincidence, just as Warren Buffet was sounding his alarm bells and the administration of President George W. Bush was grappling with the state of the world post-9/11, Matt Kelly and Craig Boyd entered the job market as graduate trainees in 2002 at Redstone Mortgage Plc, a specialised mortgage institution. Headquartered in London, the two friends were posted to the Brighton office in 2004 as an underwriter and mortgage sales officer, respectively.

In less than a decade, that is, by 2011, both their promising careers had cratered. Caught up in the windstorm that swept legions of home-owners in the US, Matt and Craig were two unwitting players in a marginal market whose lives were decisively upended.

The mythical *Masters of the Universe*, a phrase coined by the American author Tom Wolfe in his best-selling book *The Bonfire of the Vanities*, had conspired to spin a silky financial web that precipitated a momentous boom-and-bust economic cycle. As nations and businesses picked through the financial rubble, a majority of complicit Wall Street titans (a glaring exception personified by *Bernard Madoff*) made off like bandits. In such a rigged system, several bigwigs were so deep in the scandal that they could have been wearing scuba diving masks.

Perceived as being *too big to fail*, governments had little choice but to bail out the same institutions that destabilised the financial markets. And because white-collar crimes are notoriously difficult to prosecute, and to prove misdeeds beyond reasonable doubt, hardly anyone of substance was tried or convicted by the criminal justice system for fraud or excessive risk-taking. This dissonance led naysayers to insist that those who spin the web, like spiders, rarely get caught up in it.

Meanwhile in the UK, the failure of *Northern Rock* in early 2008 forced the government to shake off its stupor, and drove the Newcastle-based bank into public ownership. Having borrowed heavily to fund mortgage lending during an ambitious growth spurt, *Northern Rock* became the first British bank to experience a bank run in over a century when its liquidity dried up. When the bankruptcy of *Lehman Brothers*, a large US investment bank, unfolded in September 2008, panic quickly spread across the globe.

To soothe jangled nerves, the most emblematic villain in the UK financial world was Sir Fred Goodwin, former head of the nationalised *Royal Bank of Scotland*, who was dubbed *Fred the Shred* and vilified mercilessly by the British tabloids. Later stripped of his knighthood, Goodwin's enemies noticeably failed to follow through on their comical '*off with his fred*' threat. Although Fred Goodwin and a cohort of corporate leaders presided over unprecedented wealth destruction, but treated as statistical fodder were the voiceless whose lives were eviscerated.

With this broad canvas serving as a backdrop, on a sombre day in August 2011, Matt set out for Her Majesty's Coroner for Brighton &

Hove, the venue of the inquest into the death of his erstwhile companion, Craig. Silent as the tomb, Matt drove the five odd miles from home towards Lewes Road, Brighton. Behind the steering wheel, his mind whirled and twirled, and soon conveyed him to a much happier, less complicated period in his life.

CHAPTER 2

In the summer of 2002, Matt Kelly completed his master's degree in finance and, within three months, had been recruited by Redstone Mortgage Plc, a recent entrant into the *FTSE 250*. Within fifteen years of its incorporation, Redstone had become a recognised brand among the second tier of publicly-quoted companies listed on the London Stock Exchange.

On the first day of the induction programme at Redstone's training centre in west London, Matt arrived half an hour before the starting time of 9:00 a.m. Following the registration protocol, he walked into the plush auditorium where he easily spotted the tent card bearing his name. Already seated at the same desk was a beaming associate, who rose and evenly held out an outstretched hand,

"Howdy! I'm Craig Boyd."

"Matt Kelly… good to meet you."

As the auditorium filled up, Craig engaged Matt on a range of subjects, as only a fast-talking, half-American 'import', as he described himself, could manage. Born two months apart in 1978, but separated by five thousand miles, Matt learnt that Craig's American father and English mother were living in Austin, Texas at the time. Craig's parents divorced before his twelfth birthday and, while his oilman father remained behind in the US, his mother returned to England with Craig and his younger sister, Holly. After completing his undergraduate degree in the UK, he attended the University of Texas for his master's degree in business administration.

Almost as reserved as Craig was gregarious, Matt could barely get a word in sideways, which suited him perfectly. He discovered that he enjoyed listening to Craig, who had a lingering Texan accent. Craig informed him that thirty-six new trainees were being inducted that day at Redstone, and Matt could tell that his new acquaintance was mightily proud to be one of them. Just as Craig finally paused to catch his breath, they were interrupted by the thumping guitar chords of *Oasis*'s 1995 hit song *Wonderwall*. Several octaves louder than the *muzak* that had hitherto seeped through the surrounding walls, *Wonderwall*'s opening lyrics were a jarring introduction to Redstone's corporate culture and its chief executive, Paul Slade.

When Paul, as he immediately asked to be called, strode to the front of the auditorium, the shock of his presence at an event to welcome graduate trainees was greeted by muffled gasps of recognition. He was soon joined by two other C-level executives – from finance and marketing – as well as the human resources director, none of whom looked a day older than forty years.

After introductions were over, Paul launched into a rallying speech aimed squarely at greenhorns with scant knowledge of the housing market:

"*In a recent speech on minority home ownership, President George W. Bush said:*

'We can put light where there's darkness, and hope where there's despondency. And part of it is working together as a nation to encourage folks to own their own home.'

At Redstone, we believe that building a free society should be anchored not just on the middle class, but also on lower-income home owners. Home ownership inspires pride in people who have a vested interest in their local communities. It promotes financial stability, and enables individuals to own personal portfolios that could be passed on to future generations.

Mind you, I'm also in favour of stock ownership. Well, how could I not be, knowing how well Redstone's has performed on the stock exchange? However, the real estate market has always been the mainstay of our economy. Also, historically, tangible bricks-and-mortar assets have been considered excellent investment vehicles.

This year, the rate of owner-occupier households in the UK is touching 70%, which affirms the old adage that an Englishman's home is his castle. Our research shows that people who earn more than £12,000 but less than £25,000 face the greatest barriers – too rich for social housing but too poor for the mortgage lenders.

At Redstone, our ultimate goal is to build an acclaimed and socially-conscious company that assists hard-working but disadvantaged home buyers to get on the property ladder."

The second half of Paul's address was titled *Tougher Than The Rest*. The PowerPoint presentation highlighted the vision, mission, core values, and the corporate objectives of Redstone. Laced with graphics, each PowerPoint slide emphasised what Paul described as the entrepreneurial and can-do spirit embedded in the founders' DNA. Unapologetic about its trailblazing and 'no holds barred' culture, Paul formally welcomed the twenty-five male and eleven female *Rolling Stones* (as the company's employees were nicknamed by the media) to Redstone.

As Paul Slade took his final question and left the podium with his lieutenants, *Bruce Springsteen*'s overt tune *Tougher Than The Rest* capped what had undoubtedly been a rock star performance. From that moment onwards, a succession of presenters ran through the agenda *without* music. Most were senior managers from marketing and sales, mortgage lending, and underwriting departments who, without exception, conveyed the essence of Redstone's hard-charging credo. Soon, it was apparent that the majority of the trainees were hired primarily to boost Redstone's business expansion.

Orchestrated to foster optimum bonding, the newbies were all accommodated in a nearby hotel for the two-week duration. Interspersed with role plays, quizzes, field trips, dinners and team activities, it was all a rather heady initiation at one of the most captivating, fastest-growing companies in the UK.

Fortuitously, not only were Matt and Craig paired together in the lecture hall but they were also assigned adjoining hotel rooms. And Craig being Craig, he insisted that the connecting door between them should stay unlatched. Wryly amused, Matt consented since a part of him was intrigued by his half-Yank neighbour. Before long, Craig could identify all his other colleagues by name and, had there been a leadership contest, no doubt he would have been a top contender.

As the days wore on, the fact that Craig had interned at a US mortgage firm before joining Redstone gave him a unique perspective on the residential mortgage market that most of his colleagues lacked. Never shy to express himself, Craig did not hesitate to question or challenge the views of several of their instructors.

On the social front, a huge reception was held for the trainees at the hotel's banquet hall the second Saturday after their arrival. To enliven the occasion, each trainee was allowed one external guest and, once again, all the Redstone big guns graced the event to emphasise their commitment to the company's future.

It was early days, yet Matt could not help but notice that Craig was hitting the cocktails rather hard. Although disguised by his irrepressible zest, Matt sensed that his friend had started to slur his words by the time he got on the dais to render a karaoke song. Stealing the show with his air guitar, Craig's energetic cover of Thin Lizzy's song *Whiskey In The Jar* was unforgettable. Was Craig, subconsciously, perhaps questioning why the booze was being served in bottles rather than in *jar-os*?

On the last day of the onboarding process, the head of business strategy at Redstone, Larry Baines, provided an analysis of the state of the world. He reminded the trainees about the first anniversary of the 9/11 attacks and the US military's subsequent invasion and eviction of the Taliban and Al Qaeda from Afghanistan. Nevertheless, the world was still in the grip of the so-called 'war on terror,' which had Saddam Hussein of Iraq in the crosshairs of the US and its coalition partners.

Larry then followed up with a summary of Francis Fukuyama's controversial *The End of History and the Last Man* thesis. Fukuyama's basic argument was that, with the collapse of the Soviet Union and the end of the *Cold War*, Western liberal democracy represented an unassailable final form of human government. Without openly disputing Fukuyama's views, Larry expressed the opinion that, after seventy decades, terrorism might replace Communism as the geo-political threat to the world order. While the foreign policy arena remained turbulent, Larry felt that there appeared to be more convergence on the economic front. The US had enjoyed a historical economic boom during the Clinton years and Communist China had come out of the cold by embracing the market economy.

Lastly, Larry touched upon the *dot-com* bust at the turn of the century that saw the collapse of many Internet start-ups. Despite the stock market shakeout, the impact of information technology on productivity improvement had been remarkable. From Redstone's perspective, the monetary and regulatory liberalisation that began during Clinton's presidency galvanised a credit boom and growth opportunities in the housing market.

Reflecting on some of the earlier presentations, the cynic in Matt could not help but notice how clichéd they seemed. He happened to be a political junkie; as such, he had his own personal, perhaps more jaundiced view about how national self-interests often collided in the real world, as opposed to a picturesque outlook.

Brought back from his reverie, Matt realised that Larry was close to wrapping up his presentation. Clearly, Redstone was a company infused with optimism and dynamism. Intent on not merely succeeding but, driven by a strong winning mentality, Larry's last slide channelled Redstone's piercing rallying cry:

"HE WHO DARES WINS!"

CHAPTER 3

By late 2004, Redstone's batch of trainees had successfully navigated the company's highly immersive management development programme. Over the two-year duration, each trainee was rotated through every business unit, including spending short stints in the legal and human resources management departments.

At their 'graduation' ceremony, Paul Slade was on hand to congratulate each of the newly minted *Rolling Stones* with a handshake and a broad grin. Special prizes and awards were also distributed. Amongst these, Craig received an excellence award for 'enterprise and creativity.' Notably, Craig was the only one to share a hug and backslap with Paul, who seemed unclear as to who initiated what. After Paul's closing exhortations, the HR director joined him on stage and proceeded to hand out deployment letters to all 36 associates.

Normally a topic of speculation and high anticipation, a committee of business unit heads met to review the profile and assess the performance of the trainees. Posting recommendations were then presented to top management for a final decision.

Matt was posted to the underwriting department while Craig, to his great delight, ended up at marketing and sales. While the majority of his colleagues were assigned solely to retail mortgage lending, by virtue of his exposure to the US mortgage market, Craig was also included in the team of brokers and consultants that oversaw the wholesale sales function. Much earlier than would have been expected for such a young company, Redstone dipped its toes in the wholesale or secondary mortgage market. Through this process, loans from the primary market are pooled and sold on to pension funds, insurance companies, and investment banks as mortgage-backed securities or collateralised mortgage obligations, as described earlier. This enabled Redstone to take the loans off its balance-sheet, thereby enhancing its leverage and return on investments.

In the previous five years, Redstone had grown its loan volume at an average rate of 12% per annum. Compounded, this was phenomenal in a traditionally staid industry that barely notched 4% annually. A breakdown of the approved deployment list of the new Redstone associates showed that eighteen, or 50%, were assigned to marketing and sales. They represented the frontline troops tasked with generating sales leads, educating prospective borrowers on loan options, and assisting them through the loan origination process. Five new personnel were posted to the underwriting function, while operations, closing, post-closing and loan servicing functions had altogether a total of seven. Meanwhile, strategy, customer service, investor relations, collateral management, loan default, and portfolio and credit risk business units each received exactly one staff.

To suggest that Redstone had been on a tear would be an understatement. The head of marketing and sales, Brad Kuhn, did not mince his words when he was formally introduced to Craig and others on whom Redstone would depend to maintain the company's hot streak. Although all staff could expect a quarterly bonus based on job performance, those in marketing and sales had the added incentive of top-up commissions if they exceeded very tough sales targets.

Expounded Brad Kuhn,

"For the foreseeable future, the Bank of England projects a favourable macroeconomic

environment characterised by steady economic growth, low interest rate, moderate inflation and rising prosperity. Deregulation and the lowering of barriers translate to fierce competition, implying that there will be winners and losers. We are in a land grab situation, and market share is the name of the game.

To remain on our winning trajectory at Redstone, we have adopted an innovative approach that leverages cutting-edge technology. Furthermore, we combine extensive knowledge of the housing market with a high-risk appetite. In other words, we have evolved into a highly-integrated, well-tuned organisation that is not only very responsive but seeks opportunities where others may fear to explore.

In conclusion, ours is a noble cause. We exist to serve both the privileged and the disadvantaged in our society. Our strategic decision to become a significant player in the wholesale market ensures that we are able to borrow short, create liquidity and thus lend long, in order to fuel the growth of our residential mortgage lending portfolio."

Reading between the lines, there was an element of hubris in Brad Kuhn's summation. By promoting growth at all costs, and de-emphasising risk management, the seed of Redstone's future crisis was being sown. In 2004, Redstone was ostensibly a young company on a roll, and was yet to face serious adversity. Inside the company, many believed that traditional building societies and less successful rivals were too stodgy in a fast-moving business environment.

Looking back, the bursting of the dot-com bubble and memories of Enron and other accounting scandals had begun to recede. Thereafter, the March to November 2001 economic recession was quite mild by historical standards. Thus, by the beginning of 2005, another steadily inflating economic bubble, centred on sub-prime mortgage lending, was emerging. In this scenario, stock markets were booming and major economic indices were quite benign. For Craig and other young guns inside Redstone, they simply could not wait to hit the ground running.

In short order, Craig developed a customised sales presentation, which he rehearsed in the apartment he shared with Matt. As Craig was always quick to point out, his unit was the most important at Redstone since it initiated the mortgage life cycle. Whereas the prime or topflight market constituted well over 70% of Redstone's portfolio, the real battleground for marketing and sales was the vibrant, though more risky, sub-prime sector.

The established channels for reaching new customers included Redstone's main branch in Brighton, by telephone, and through the Internet. In his primary sales role, Craig was expected to contribute towards the growth of Redstone's mortgage loan portfolio by identifying, developing and maintaining a network of relationships to facilitate mortgage lending opportunities. Daily, he had to make sales calls to prospective customers, examine incoming applications and supporting documentation, evaluate credit-worthiness and repayment risk, and ultimately close deals. Also, by reaching out to the wider Brighton & Hove community of real estate professionals, builders, and participating in local efforts to increase home ownership, he was able to build a valuable mailing list.

Soon, Craig would swing into action by leveraging his financial skills and grasp of Redstone's business applications. But to earn the trust of prospective borrowers, his natural charm was an invaluable asset when he made that most important first contact, either face-to-face or through cold calls. At 6ft-4in, Craig was quite a life force whose bonhomie left an indelible impression on most people who crossed his path. When the spirit moved him, it was not unheard of that Craig would hug new acquaintances. His impact at the Brighton branch was immediate and unabashed. He was the archetypal proselytizer Redstone needed to burnish its brand in a crowded field of local rivals.

Unlike Craig, Matt was office-bound in a circumspect role in the mortgage underwriting department. Primarily, the department evaluated and verified loan application details such as income information and credit history. By assessing the applicant's assets and collaterals, and determining the capacity to repay the mortgage loan, Matt's business unit had the responsibility to approve or deny loan applications. Traditionally, application processing in the mortgage industry was largely manual. However, advances in information technology introduced automated underwriting, encompassing credit scoring and affordability assessment – a capability that Redstone introduced before many of its competitors.

Located in South East England, the Brighton housing market was influenced by several factors. As a coastal city with a population of about 270,000, and within an hour from central London by rail, Brighton has always attracted its fair share of commuters, immigrants, and young people. Significantly, the owner-occupier rate of 62% within Brighton & Hove in 2005 was lower than in the adjoining regions of East Sussex and West Sussex. Furthermore, the stock of flats and apartments relative to detached and semi-detached properties was much higher in the former area than the latter.

As Craig and his new colleagues digested local and regional housing data, they discovered that the average price of a flat in central Brighton had gone up from about £48,500 in 1997 to £195,000 by 2005, representing a 300% surge. Although this upturn was not uniform across all property types, an unbroken increase in house prices was attracting not only owner-occupiers but also buy-to-let landlords and financial speculators.

The problem with this scenario was that, by 2005, the average house price-to-income ratio in the Brighton & Hove area was about six. For instance, a home buyer required £37-42,000 to purchase an entry-level flat. For a semi-detached or fully-detached house, the figure ranged from £55,000 to £75,000. In general, the income profile of Brighton & Hove residents had deteriorated over time as higher-paying jobs in the manufacturing and energy sectors were gradually replaced by jobs in the distribution, tourism, and service sectors. By 2005, just over 30% of households within the area could comfortably afford an entry-level property at those prices, including well-heeled parents who acquired one-bedroom apartments for privileged university students. Nonetheless, Craig could easily infer that aspiring first-time buyers within the sub-prime housing category represented a critical mass.

Despite the risk of default, the competition amongst mortgage lenders in the sub-prime market intensified on the assumption that property prices would continue to rise while interest rates remained benign. Within Redstone, managing the apparently conflicting objective of boosting the loan volume and controlling the risk of possible default led to growing tension between business units. Whilst underwriters were responsible for strict adherence to loan approval policies, marketers fought for a relaxation. Rather than relying on the automated process of credit scoring and underwriting when processing borderline applications, loan officers were instructed to collate such applications manually, and then to refer them to the loan committee.

In order to convince nervous or wavering loan applicants to take the plunge, loan officers courted such prospects in diverse ways. This included developing personal relationships, or by painting a rosy economic outlook. Possibly no one exemplified this hard-sell approach better than Craig Boyd. While he readily admitted to the thrill of closing new deals, he also enjoyed developing new friendships that grew out of the process. His personal touch included home visitations, pub camaraderie, and invitations to sporting events.

The case of a newly married couple, James and Kay Huntington was highly illustrative. Their combined income as at 2006 was a shade below £30,000. Wishing to acquire an apartment valued at £240,000, this implied income multiples of about 8.0. Seeing an opening, Craig courted them with all guns blazing. He wined and dined them, took his time to cultivate Kay who seemed more decisive than her husband, and kept reminding them that house prices had been rising for over a decade. Indeed, as the months ticked by, property prices continued to climb to what proved to be unsustainable levels. What finally clinched the deal was when Kay convinced James that they should defer starting a family. Instead, they solicited assistance from their parents for the initial deposit.

When Craig presented the Huntington application to the loan committee, he knew he was asking the panel to override Redstone's income multiple threshold of 6.0. In his recommendation, he highlighted the fact that James and Kay were in permanent employment with solid future prospects and, secondly, the property's location guaranteed excellent resale prospects. The committee reviewed the couple's monthly expenditure statement and, despite the evident risk, the application was approved and Craig promptly closed the deal.

From the second quarter of 2005 through to the spring of 2008, Redstone ran like a well-oiled machine. The sub-prime loan volume grew briskly, thanks to the efforts of those closest to the coal face. Well-rewarded for his endeavours through stock options and bonuses, Craig did well enough to enable him to make a deposit for a maisonette in a high-value residential area. Six months afterwards, Matt followed suit by purchasing an apartment within the same complex. Instead of renting, both friends became proud property owners with twenty-five year mortgages underwritten by Redstone.

Although a few *Cassandras* in the US were beginning to sound alarm bells about the threat posed by a credit bubble, other experts believed that the dragon of the business cycle had been tamed once and for all. Another influential group promoted the efficient market hypothesis which claims that prices of traded assets, such as stocks and property, fully reflect all publicly available information. Risks were already baked-in and, in a low-inflation environment, surely it was sweetness and light all the way.

In such a climate, what on earth could possibly go wrong?

CHAPTER 4

Matt pulled into the parking lot of the Coroner's court, stepped out and slowly walked towards the entrance. Consumed with grief and regret, he shuddered at the thought of giving evidence in the death of a colleague and companion.

In a queue that had slowly formed at the reception desk, Matt spotted Craig's father, Skip Boyd, and his daughter, Holly, signing the register. Craig's mother had been so distraught at his funeral that it did not surprise him that she skipped the inquest. After signing in, he was given an agenda sheet by the court usher, who then steered him to a waiting room reserved for the family and friends of the deceased. At the top of the agenda sheet was the name of the Coroner – Mr. John McDougal, below which were listed the following: the date of the inquest, the time, the name of the deceased, age, date of death, and place of death.

The Boyds hugged Matt in turn before he sat next to Mr. Boyd, who was struggling to mask his emotions. Speaking first, Skip said,

"*Good to see you, Matt. How have you been?*"

"*Very well… thank you, sir. When did you arrive?*"

"*I flew in on a direct flight from Dallas two days ago… And thanks for all your support.*"

Spotting Craig's former housekeeper, Matt whispered,

"*Be right back. Let me say hello to Mrs. Keegan.*"

Not that she was superstitious, but Ellen Keegan had told Matt that an unusually heavy sea mist covered Brighton roads as she made her way to work that morning. She had discovered Craig's body when she arrived at her usual time of 10:00 a.m. Panicked, she had alerted Matt who then took charge on a horrible day that still seemed surreal.

Minutes after greeting Mrs. Keegan, Matt returned to the Boyds and sat next to Holly. As they chatted, he noticed that the surrounding wall was painted a dour colour that was, frankly, migraine-inducing. With Holly struggling to hold back tears, the room turned slightly cooler when the usher

31

threw open the double door and invited them into the courtroom. When everyone was seated, the court clerk, who wore a suit of no easy description, ran through formal instructions printed on the back of the agenda,

"As a rule, please listen to the following dos and don'ts:

1. *Do switch off all mobile phones. And, no, do not put them on silent mode.*

2. *Do not eat, drink or chew gum.*

3. *Do rise when the Coroner arrives and leaves the courtroom.*

4. *Do not refer to the Coroner as 'Your Honour.' 'Sir' would do.*

5. *Do not wear a hat or head covering during proceedings. But exceptions could be made on religious grounds.*

Thank you. That will be all for now."

About five minutes later, the usher intoned,

"All rise."

Out of a walled-in door emerged Mr. John McDougal, Her Majesty's Coroner for Brighton & Hove. Wearing a well-trimmed beard above a pin-striped suit, but without a wig or gown, he looked every inch like a funeral director, which he was in a manner of speaking.

Speaking into a microphone, the Coroner delivered his opening remarks,

"Ladies and gentlemen, I welcome you all to the inquest into the death of Craig Newton Boyd.

Before proceeding, Her Majesty's Court extends its condolences to Mr. Boyd's immediate family, and to his former associates and friends.

For emphasis, let me declare that an inquest is not a trial. We are not here to decide on issues of guilt, blame, or compensation. Instead, one of our key objectives is to learn lessons that will prevent future deaths from occurring. In other words, at its conclusion, no penalty or sentence will be issued by the Coroner.

I would describe this process as a fact-finding inquiry that will provide a detailed account to establish who died, how, when and where.

Based on the full investigative report submitted to the Coroner's Office and the prevailing circumstances, it was decided that this inquest did not warrant a jury.

I estimate that this inquest should last about two days. If everything runs on time, we should conclude by mid-afternoon or latest by 5:00 p.m. tomorrow.

According to the roster in front of me, six witnesses are scheduled to make statements. Each of you will be called to the witness box, and will take an oath to provide true evidence. I will ask questions, if necessary, and members of the family and other interested parties who have been pre-selected can also ask questions. I repeat, please bear in mind that this is not a trial. Therefore, questions should be asked only for clarification, not in an adversarial cross-examination manner.

We also have two legal representatives – one for the family and the other from Redstone Mortgage Plc, the former employer of the deceased. Each of them will address the Coroner before the verdict is rendered.

If there are any questions, please liaise with the court clerk. Thank you.

Clerk, please call the first witness."

As the inquest kicked off, hanging in the air like a dark cloud was why a successful 33-year old professional died so prematurely.

Essentially, the period 2002-07 represented an almost synchronised economic boom across the world, including in developing countries. Globally, the boost in credit flows pushed the cost of capital down, leading to an underestimation of risk. In the housing market in particular, it was a well-established fact that sub-prime borrowers who would not be considered creditworthy under normal prudential standards were deemed to be profitable and worthy targets by yield-seeking operators. To be frank, some borrowers who fell into this category were either gullible or deceitful. To entice these risky borrowers, financial institutions offered various inducements, such as low initial payments for the first few years. With this trend, 48% of new mortgage originations in the US – the epicentre of the market – were sub-prime by 2006.

The near-unanimous optimism about the state of the global economy in 2006 seduced many people into ignoring the warning signs. These included the upswing in housing and equity prices, loose US monetary policy which fuelled the credit boom, the rising level of private debts, and the exposure of lenders and investors to unprecedented levels of securitisation of mortgages.

Before 2000, very few mortgage lenders in the UK had used credit scoring or credit reference agency data. And even fewer had been exposed to securitisation. However, by 2005, the majority were either fully automated or partially automated. Using standardised criteria, over 20% of mortgage applicants were refused credit by mainstream institutions, thus providing a ready market for sub-prime lenders.

By 2006, the looming collapse of the US housing market could be traced to the US central bank, the Federal Reserve, which began to gradually increase interest rates in an attempt to moderate the credit boom. The brake on introductory low interest rates on sub prime loans also marked the beginning in delinquency on home loans. This development picked up momentum into 2007 and led to the failure of some US mortgage lenders. As the level of defaults grew, it emerged that banks, insurance companies, and other investors were equivocal about their levels of exposure due to the complex nature of the financial products, mainly CDOs and CDSs, on their books.

This led directly to the reluctance of financial institutions to lend to each other, causing markets to freeze up. As the element of trust and interbank lending evaporated, the rescue of the US investment bank, Bear Stearns, in early 2008 and the subsequent bankruptcy of Lehman Brothers with liabilities topping $600 billion in September 2008, brought the crisis to a head. In the US, well over 20 banks had failed by the end of 2008. To make matters worse, the sharp rise in oil prices in 2008, reaching a peak of $147 per barrel, caused worldwide fears of a trade recession.

In early 2009, George W. Bush took his exit and the new US President Barack Obama was determined to steady the US economy, with no guarantee of success. Seeking to avoid mistakes made by policy makers during previous crises, the G20 (forum of the world's 20 largest advanced and emerging economies) reacted decisively by injecting massive amounts of liquidity into financial markets and nationalising banks, slashing interest rates, and increasing discretionary spending through fiscal stimulus packages. This response helped to foil a catastrophic depression in many countries.

In the UK, the ensuing credit crunch triggered market volatility which exposed vulnerable borrowers in the sub-prime mortgage sector to grave difficulties, such as missed mortgage payments or adverse county court judgments. Elsewhere, the Bradford & Bingley Building Society was effectively nationalised in late 2008, followed by the partial nationalisation of the Royal Bank of Scotland. Meanwhile the UK's largest mortgage lender, Halifax Bank of Scotland (HBOS) was forced to merge with the Lloyds Group before the UK government took a sizeable stake in the combined entity. Even as central banks valiantly cut interest rates, interbank interest rates remained stubbornly high thus further tightening the credit markets, and deepening the downturn in the construction and housing markets.

Redstone, a leading mortgage lender, experienced a sharp contraction in its lending capacity, which fell by as much as 80% in 2009. The company's inability to access the wholesale markets for funding piled on the additional pressure, even as the number of borrowers in arrears and negative equity soared. Having pushed income multiples and average loan-to-value ratios to the extremes, the unanticipated credit crunch hit the company hard. Instead of growth as a strategy, default management became the key preoccupation. To stem the bleeding, Redstone tried to help distressed borrowers through forbearance and loan restructuring, which were deemed preferable to mortgage possession.

People at greatest risk were those who bought properties at the height of the market, including individuals who became unemployed and found it difficult to find ready buyers, in order to pay off their loans. There were also couples who made purchases based on combined incomes but whose relationships subsequently broke down. And, of course, there were multitudes who simply could no longer meet their loan obligations.

To forestall the wave of potential mortgage possessions, the UK government took a series of actions. This included assistance with mortgage-interest payments; the introduction of a *Mortgage Rescue Scheme* whereby struggling borrowers could sell their properties to housing associations while paying rent and continuing to live in them, and also through a reduction in bank rates by the Bank of England. Despite these interventions, the rate of possessions in 2009 was five times higher than in 2004. The chaos was made worse due to mutual recrimination between mortgage lenders and borrowers, as well as internal tension within lending institutions like Redstone that had never experienced a housing market bust.

Ever the optimist, who was yet to face any serious setback in life, Craig kept hoping that 2008 was just a dip. He was on the phone to his father almost every night, seeking reassurance. But as it slowly dawned on Craig that the contagion from the US was global, his world seemed to collapse around him. As the downturn intensified, he struggled with the new normal of daily visits and phone calls from frightened and angry customers.

On one of several visits to Matt's apartment during this period, Craig wore his concerns on his sleeves. They talked about little else but the economic recession, the housing market, and their future at Redstone.

"Can you believe that I've been receiving all kinds of threats lately?" said Craig, as he paced the room, fidgeting and looking extremely agitated.

"Really? That sounds awful."

"I am being called everything from stupid to incompetent. One man actually threatened me with knee-capping... Oh, and let's not forget the slur that seems to be on everyone's lips: 'you are a fraud'," added Craig.

"Have you shared any of this with your line manager?" asked Matt.

Craig nodded dejectedly.

"And?"

"Nothing much. At our weekly meetings, we're told to hang in there, and that it will all blow over once the dust settles.

Honestly, I'm not so sure about that. This crisis appears different somehow... no one seems to have any cogent answer..."

Just as Craig sensed, Redstone's management seemed to be in denial. Instead of developing a unified message and talking points, the primary focus was on how to stem the collapse of the company's stock price. To lower the temperature, even the most delinquent borrowers were offered restructuring plans. But many of these sub-prime customers simply turned their ire on

Redstone's marketers who they blamed for railroading them into taking the loans in the first place.

Matt noticed that his friend's sunny disposition was progressively turning dark. Knowing how much Craig fed off others' approval and affection, Matt feared that he was succumbing to anxiety and depression. Mind you, Matt was also struggling with his own demons. The underwriting department had continually been undermined in its assigned roles. Its most crucial role was the assessment of an applicant's capability to service and repay the loan applied for and, second, the appraisal of the adequacy of the property being offered as security or collateral for the loan. Very often, the loan committee – made up of senior executives – overruled underwriters and sided with loan officers, who were desperate to meet their quarterly targets.

Far from being naïve, Matt sensed all along that Redstone's understaffing of both the collateral management and the portfolio/credit risk departments finally came back to bite the company. Weak internal controls during the boom years now seemed imprudent at best, and utterly reckless in a worst-case scenario.

Rather than subsiding, the pressure on Redstone grew. Unable to access the wholesale market for funding, its loan portfolio shrank even as the level of default increased. By the beginning of 2010, its share price was nearly 70% off its peak. This meant that employees' stock options were now under water and could therefore not be vested. Simultaneously, with bonuses evaporating, staff morale fell like a stone. By then, Craig had taken to heavy drinking and had begun to consume prescription drugs for his anxiety attacks. Occasionally, he would show up in the office unshaven and worse for wear. Unlike some of his colleagues who viewed the situation through a corporate prism, to Craig, it was very personal indeed.

As time passed, Craig became less communicative and admitted that he was not sleeping well. Whenever they were together, Matt noticed that his mood swung from sullen to silent. Later, Matt became truly worried when Craig's live-in girlfriend, Nancy Gibbs, moved out of their apartment. Emotionally, she claimed to have hit a brick wall due to Craig's chronic drinking and feared that he was on a downward spiral. Not knowing what else to do, Matt contacted Craig's mother and sister in the UK who, in turn, introduced

Matt to Craig's US-based father, Skip. By then, Craig's eating disorder had led to creeping weight loss and lethargy. While Craig's family was evaluating all options, Matt took a radical decision.

A sudden brainwave propelled him to send an e-mail highlighting Craig's plight to Redstone's CEO, senior executives, Brighton branch staff, and he also blind-copied Craig. However, he might as well have broadcast it to all Redstone employees (a privilege reserved to only C-level executives) because, by the end of that work day, it had been forwarded and re-forwarded countless times to every nook and cranny of Redstone. To suggest that Matt set off a firestorm would be a gross understatement.

The e-mail read:

"Date: 08 February 2011

Re: Craig Boyd Mayday

My Fellow Stones,

Like many of my colleagues, I have been living through an ordeal that was triggered by what Nassim Taleb described as a 'black swan' – a once-in-decades event that almost no one saw coming.

Let's admit it, just about everyone was blindsided by the sudden downturn in the housing market.

We thought we had a winning hand which we played to the hilt - until the bottom fell out. Truth be told, we were all culpable in the pursuit of growth at all costs, and it would have taken real guts to speak up about our lax internal controls and risk management procedures while the company was steamrolling its competitors.

Now, let me turn to why I decided to write this e-mail.

Our colleague, and my friend, Craig Boyd, has been flaming out for months into a depressive funk. I would describe him, and others caught up in this mess, as being mousetrapped. Emotionally, Craig has been grappling with the damage the property crisis has inflicted on many of his clients.

In retrospect, Craig now believes that the majority of the loans that he originated should never have been made in the first place. No doubt, that is an extremely controversial assertion by a Redstone employee. But that is a true reflection of his state of mind. Medically, the NHS is doing its best for Craig but I'm afraid it may be inadequate.

I am aware that my mode of intervention is unconventional but I urge management to please act to rescue Craig before it is too late.

Best regards,

Matt Kelly"

CHAPTER 5

Until the weekend created an artificial dam, Matt's inbox overflowed with e-mails from Redstone locations across the UK:

"Are you f_____ serious?"

"Way to go, Matt."

"Kudos!"

"Man, how dare you s__ where you eat?"

"Ouch!"

"Who do you think you are?"

"Thumbs up!"

"Who gives a d__ about your 'friend'?"

"FU!"

"Why are you p___ down your trouser leg?"

"Traitor!"

"Team spirit, loyalty, anyone?"

"*Yo, is anyone listening?*"

"*Let's have a drink.*"

"*Egregious.*"

"*My hero!*"

"*J-d-s*"

Mind you, these were just the one-liners. Some responses were longer than Matt's original message.

Rather sanguine about it all, Matt's most fascinating, and meaningful, exchange was with Craig:

"*Thanks for sticking up for me, Matt. Much appreciated... but I have to ask you one question.*"

"*Shoot... at least I got you talking.*"

"*There you go again. But, seriously, what did you mean by 'mousetrapped'?*"

"*Ah, what do I really know? But here's what springs to mind.*

First, did the mouse at least get the cheese? If yes, then it should swallow.

Second, did the trap catch its tail? If yes, then it should jerk like crazy, and try to escape.

Third, did the trap strike flesh? If yes, then the mouse should start praying and prepare to fast."

"Ha-ha! That's helpful... you always have a way of cheering me up. But, unlike you, I have only one recurring interpretation."

"Let's hear it..."

"Don't laugh, OK?

We – you and I – are certified 'Stones,' right? Imagine what happens if we end up inside a cannon. Well, there is only one way out, isn't there?"

"You mean, getting fired? Is that what's been eating you up?" Matt sounded incredulous.

"Partly, but also I feel so guilty about all the folks who have been hurt. I've never had to deal with a situation where I feel so helpless."

"Craig, for goodness' sake! This is a global financial crisis... You can't shoulder all the blame. That's absurd!

Please, please, can you at least promise me that you'll stop drinking so much... before you harm yourself?"

In response, Craig sighed forlornly and slowly looked away.

Back at Redstone, Matt had touched a nerve among the workforce. But, ultimately, what really mattered was how Redstone's top management would react.

As incendiary as Matt's *Mayday* e-mail was, the truth was that the company's survival was uppermost on management's mind. 2010 had been a complete disaster, a year that ended with takeover speculation of Redstone by a competitor. To have any hope of retaining its independence, the company needed to unwind and clean up its portfolio, which was proving difficult to implement in a depressed market. For starters, Redstone needed to downsize in the short-term to shrink its overhead expenditure. Although reducing the payroll would not guarantee a successful turnaround, it would at least send the right signal to the stock market and outside investors.

A fly on the wall at Redstone's weekly executive management meeting in London the following Tuesday would have confirmed the company's top priorities. Expectedly, there was general banter about Matt's e-mail prior to the start of the meeting. But, in reality, this was a hard-nosed bunch driven by the bottom line. Culturally, co-founder Paul Slade did not set out to build a touchy-feely company, but rather a pace-setting market leader. An occasional marathoner, his attitude was that Redstone had hit an unexpected bump in the road but nothing, absolutely nothing was going to destroy his dream.

Incidentally, at the top of this meeting's agenda was a proposal to reduce the headcount by 25% in the next fiscal year, starting April 2011. Inputs had been collated from all the branches, including the corporate office (Paul would later insist on raising that figure to 30%). Agenda item 5 was a discussion of Matt's e-mail, but when eagled-eyed Paul spotted Craig's and Matt's names in the Brighton retrenchment list, he urged the meeting to address both issues at once.

Before the phantom fly, by then hungry and parched, left the meeting room, its feat of espionage had borne fruit. The group's consensus was that the fortuitous receipt of Matt's *Mayday* e-mail precluded them from firing Craig and Matt at that moment. The matter would be referred to the company's legal department, and its recommendation would be tabled and addressed in a fortnight's time.

Redstone's lawyers had been extremely busy since the crisis erupted, interfacing with regulators, investors, and the courts, among others. Therefore, the challenge posed by Matt's e-mail represented an awkward distraction. Redstone's highly experienced general counsel, Leslie Howe, chuckled as he read Matt's e-mail. Mousetrapped!?! He found the syntax rather unusual and wondered whether the author could be a potential whistle-blower. His job was to anticipate trouble and to protect Redstone's interests.

Worryingly, his department's resources were stretched to breaking point and he had barely two weeks to report back to Paul. Before doing so, he needed to learn as much as possible about Matt Kelly and Craig Boyd. Instantly, he decided to hire a private investigating firm that he knew would handle the assignment with the highest discretion.

While Craig was too despondent to take notice, Matt could swear that he was being followed on his way to and from the office, although he could not prove it. Once, he made an abrupt U-turn without signalling, but the 'tailing' vehicle simply drove on, not quite like in the movies. He also suspected that his apartment might have been searched when he was away at work. However, Matt could not share his concern with anyone, wary of fanning the flame of his paranoia. Around the office, colleagues ribbed him about his minor celebrity but he also sensed that some were ill at ease around him, while a few avoided making eye contact.

When the job cuts were announced in late February 2011, on a Friday, just about everyone was taken by surprise. About three out of every ten employees were being axed, skewed more towards the north and Midlands compared to the south. Altogether, the staff strength in the Brighton area was reduced by 23%. But buried deep in the cascading news was the fate of Craig and Matt.

That evening, Matt went over to Craig's apartment to discuss what had just happened. They had chatted briefly in the office, but now they had ample time to swap their official letters.

First, Craig's:

"25 February 2011

Dear Mr. Boyd,

This is to inform you that you have been placed on administrative leave, effective 01 March, 2011.

We hope you will use this opportunity to resolve the health issues that you are currently experiencing. After six months, we shall review your situation.

In the meantime, you shall be entitled to your full salary and benefits.

Please be informed that you are expected to participate in the annual strategy webinar featuring our chief executive, Paul Slade, on 28 March 2011 to mark the end of this fiscal year.

If you need any clarification, please do not hesitate to contact your People Manager.

Yours sincerely,

HR Manager

Then, Matt's:

"25 February 2011

Dear Mr. Kelly,

Due to the well-known challenges sweeping our industry, and the need to reorganise internally, the shortage of work has compelled us to place you on an indefinite administrative suspension, effective 01 March, 2011.

In the meantime, you shall be entitled to half your salary and commensurate benefits.

If you need any clarification, please do not hesitate to contact your People Manager.

Yours sincerely,

HR Manager

Matt's first thought was that this letter was likely to aggravate Craig's neurosis. Callously, management simply sidestepped Matt's e-mail and plunged right ahead with its retrenchment plans. After a minute of studied silence, Matt asked,

"So, what do you think?"

"I'm very upset. It seems to me that the company is trying to cut me loose. Almost as if I've become a monkey on their backs…," responded Craig, as his train of thought ran cold.

"Hmm… Clearly, my e-mail was swatted aside. Redstone is refusing to take any responsibility for your care and recovery.

Now, I don't necessarily believe in coincidences… but I can't help feeling that I could easily have been fired outright; but the company stayed its hand to avoid any potential liability. By suspending me, I end up in limbo… in no man's land."

"Same here. It feels like being in purgatory… being hung out to dry. They've given themselves six months of breathing space, following which the company might well find a justification to ease me out."

"In other words, you could say that our days at Redstone are numbered, or that we are living on borrowed time. Meanwhile, I continue to receive distressing phone calls from my mortgage clients.

This fellow called to inform me about how his house was possessed by Redstone, after he missed four consecutive payments. He'd lost his job and his savings had almost dried up. He asked me what he should do. Another guy told me that his wife was threatening to leave with the kids for her parents' if they lost their house. As you can imagine, I had absolutely nothing to offer them...," Craig lamented.

"Honestly, I suspect that it's going to get much worse before it gets better. The global economy is tanking, but the hope is that the co-ordinated impact of the stimulus packages proposed by the G20, China and other nations will soon steady the ship. But I suspect we should expect a long period of austerity now that the Tories, backed by the Lib Dems, are back in power.

You know what... I think we both need a break – away from Brighton. I spoke to your sister, Holly, a few weeks ago. I think it would be a good idea if you spent some time with her family. I plan to be away in Paris to visit my fiancé for a couple of weeks. Well, since you need to be in the office on Monday, 28th March, I'll schedule my arrival for that weekend. What do you say?"

"Sounds like a good idea. Technically, I am still an employee of Redstone; so, I cannot pursue a new job offer... well, not that jobs are going begging right now. Anyway, for now, visiting Holly and Brad in Devon makes perfect sense... haven't seen them and their kids in ages."

"I'm glad we got that settled. I should be off by Wednesday. If I don't see you before then, please extend my regards to Holly and Brad. See you in about three weeks' time."

Incredibly, and sadly, that was the last time Matt would see his friend alive.

CHAPTER 6

Before she read out her statement in court, Mrs. Keegan took an oath to tell the truth, in case she had to give oral evidence on the basis of the statement. After settling down in the witness box, the Coroner gave her the nod to begin:

"I am Ellen Keegan, a domestic housekeeper employed by a private cleaning company, Pristine Limited, at Wilmot Road, Portslade, Brighton BN43 6NE. I have worked at Pristine for about five years.

On 3rd May 2010, I started working as a housekeeper at Apartment 7, 4 Montpelier Road, Brighton, BN1 3BB, the residence of Mr. Craig Boyd.

My duties included cleaning the two-bedroom apartment and doing the laundry every Monday, between 10:00 a.m. and 02:00 p.m. I was given a spare key with which I always let myself into the apartment. Normally, Mr. Boyd would have left for work by the time I arrived.

I can confirm that on the 7th, 14th, and 21st March 2011, when I arrived, Mr. Boyd was in his bedroom. He would leave his bedroom temporarily to have breakfast, and to give me space to complete the cleaning.

On Monday, 28th March 2011, I showed up as usual and let myself in at 10:02 a.m. Slumped on the long settee in the living-room was Mr. Boyd with his left arm dangling and touching the rug. At first sight, I thought that he was asleep so I instinctively called out his name several times. When he did not respond, it was then that I noticed two bottles of Jack Daniels by the settee – one was empty while the other was a quarter full. By the bottles were three smaller bottles that contained what I suspected was some medication.

Confused, I shook Mr. Boyd's right shoulder, and that was when his body slid off the settee onto the floor. At that moment, I screamed and ran out of the apartment. When I regained some composure, I recalled that Mr. Boyd had a friend who lived in a flat a floor below. Without knowing whether he would be at home or not, I ran to Mr. Kelly's front door and began banging on it.

Within a minute, based on my recollection, Mr. Kelly opened the door and came out in casual clothes. I held onto his hand and, as I dragged him *towards Mr. Boyd's flat, I must have narrated as best as I could what I had witnessed.*

When we arrived upstairs, I could not bring myself to re-enter the apartment, so Mr. Kelly went in alone.

In conclusion, that was the extent of my involvement until the arrival of the paramedics and, later, the police who took an initial statement from me."

For the record, the Coroner asked the clerk to confirm that what Mrs. Keegan read out was the signed copy in the custody of the Coroner's Office.

"Mrs. Keegan, I would like to clarify one aspect of your statement, if that's all right.

In the time leading up to the event of 28th March 2011, were there any indications to indicate whether or not the deceased had been drinking more than usual?"

"Since I'm not a trained medical personnel, I cannot give a direct answer to that question. However, I noticed in the weeks and months before March 2018, upwards of four to seven empty bottles of liquor in the trash can every Monday. I must say

that I read no meaning into this since Mr. Boyd could well have had friends over."

"OK. But, more specifically, in the early weeks of March 2018 when you stated that Mr. Boyd was in the apartment on your arrival, can you describe what state he was in when he left his bedroom," persisted the Coroner.

"He greeted me in his usual manner and there was no major change in his mood or speech pattern. The only thing I do recall is that I would retrieve one or two empty bottles of alcoholic drink from the bin in his room. On the side table by his bed, there might be a half-full bottle of drink and a glass, but my duty was simply to clean out the room, no more."

"Thank you, Mrs. Keegan."

The Coroner then asked if any of the interested parties or legal representatives had any questions for Mrs. Keegan. There was none so she was chaperoned out of the witness box.

Next up was Matt. Now, because Matt was deemed to be a crucial nexus in the life and death of Craig Boyd, a Coroner's Officer was assigned to assist him with the preparation of his statement.

This was to ensure that no crucial evidence was overlooked.

Matt's narrative began from the moment he met Craig almost a decade earlier at Redstone's onboarding event. He described very briefly the nature of the work each of them did at Redstone, leading up to the inception and aftermath of the crisis that engulfed their company and the UK economy in 2008.

As best as he could, he narrated Craig's reaction to Redstone's sudden reversal of fortune, the blowback from customers, the worsening of his drinking problem, followed by his gradual deterioration.

At that juncture, Matt asked the Coroner if he could read out the *Mayday* e-mail that he sent to Redstone's management, and to have the correspondence placed on record. Swiftly, Redstone's general counsel, Leslie Howe, who was present in court got up and asked to discuss the matter with the Coroner in private. Although this was a rather unusual intervention during an inquest, the Coroner called for a lunch break, and summoned both Mr. Howe and the legal representative of the Boyd family, Roger Kincaid, to his office.

On resumption, the Coroner announced his decision:

"After listening to Mr. Howe's argument and Mr. Kincaid's counterargument in relation to Mr. Kelly's missive – actually an e-mail that he sent to his employer, Redstone Mortgage Plc – I have come to a decision.

It is my considered opinion that, in the context and interest of establishing what may have led to the untimely death of Mr. Craig Boyd, the said e-mail written by Mr. Kelly is relevant and should be included in the public record.

At the end of the proceedings, Mr. Howe will have an opportunity to state publicly his company's viewpoint, as would the legal representative of the Boyd family, Mr. Kincaid."

With that, Matt was invited back to the witness box. After reading out the *Mayday* e-mail message, the Coroner proceeded to question him in detail about the circumstances surrounding it, and his last encounter with Craig up until 28th March.

"Was there any official feedback from Redstone to your e-mail?"

"No, Sir. But, on Monday 25th February, both Craig and I received letters informing us about our new employment status. Craig was placed on administrative leave while mine was an indefinite suspension. Mind you, hundreds of our colleagues were effectively dismissed that same day in a wave of layoffs."

"Noted. Please could you describe what happened the last time you were with the late Mr. Boyd," continued the Coroner.

"In retrospect, perhaps I missed certain cues about how Craig reacted to the letter from Redstone. Or maybe he managed to camouflage his true feelings.

The last time I saw Craig was that Monday although I called him from my mobile phone the following Wednesday on my way to Paris. He told me he would be off to Devon on Friday to stay with his sister's family. As I later discovered, Craig never left Brighton. Instead, he phoned his sister to tell her about his job situation, and that he was taking a break and would be accompanying me to Europe for three weeks.

I returned to Brighton on Sunday, 27th March around 9:30 p.m. bone-tired, and promptly went to bed. I was not certain whether Craig was back but left it to the next day to find out.

I was up and relaxing in my apartment the next morning when I heard the loud banging on the door at a little after 10:00 a.m."

At that point, the Coroner interrupted Matt,

"Can you please confirm if you found any note, letter or correspondence written by Mr. Boyd at the scene?"

"No, Sir, I did not." responded Matt.

"Then, can I suggest that you read out the rest of your statement, since it has been very carefully documented?"

Matt proceeded to describe what he discovered when he entered Craig's apartment. In shock, he felt Craig's pulse and found none. Instinctively, he turned over his friend's body and administered some CPR in an attempt to revive him, all to no avail. Grabbing his phone, he promptly called the emergency ambulance service, as well as the police. Next, he left the room briefly to comfort

Mrs. Keegan, and then ran down to the building's front desk to attract security's attention.

Within minutes after returning upstairs with the security guard, two paramedics were on the scene, followed shortly by two policemen. That, effectively, was the summation of Matt's evidence, as corroborated by the Coroner's Officer.

Matt was followed by one of the police officers present at the scene. With practised professionalism, he provided what was essentially a routine but detailed report.

At that point, the Coroner announced that the ambulance service personnel's statement would be combined with that of the doctor who performed the post-mortem on Craig. Then, the inquest was adjourned.

At 9:30 a.m. the following day, the defining moment of the inquest began when Dr. Aaron Fuqua gave his testimony. After being sworn in, he put on his reading glasses, and in a rich baritone started by stating his name, work address and professional qualifications.

Based on the report submitted by the paramedics on the scene, he described how they alighted at the deceased's home address within five minutes of being alerted. A close examination of the lifeless body of Mr. Craig Boyd confirmed that he was beyond resuscitation and had in fact been dead for several hours. Close on their tail were two police officers who arrived to take photographs and fingerprints, inventoried the living room and the deceased's bedroom, and then took statements from both Mrs. Keegan and Mr. Kelly.

Very carefully, the crucial evidence consisting of prescription pills and liquor bottles retrieved from the living room, bedroom and medication from a cabinet in the bathroom were placed in evidence bags and duly labelled. Following a nod from the police officers, Mr. Boyd's corpse was then conveyed on a gurney to the waiting ambulance and transported to the Brighton & Hove City Mortuary.

Dr. Fuqua then continued,

"*Mr. Boyd's medical records showed that he was diagnosed with depression and acute anxiety in June 2010. Consequently, he was prescribed with the antidepressant medication (or so-called selective serotonin reuptake inhibitors) Fluoxextine by his GP. Also found in Mr. Boyd's apartment were bottles of Mogadon and Valium, two tranquillisers that enhance the effect of alcohol. In the UK, these tranquillisers are available on the streets; that is, they are not illegal without a doctor's prescription. When mixed with alcohol, they can be extremely dangerous and can cause a fatal overdose.*

To ascertain the cause of Mr. Boyd's death, toxicology tests were conducted, including urine tests, to determine the types and quantities of medication in his body. The test results conclusively indicated that Mr. Boyd died from a toxic combination of alcohol poisoning and drug overdose. Because he was apparently alone in the apartment at the time, there was no immediate medical intervention that might have saved his life.

There were no signs whatsoever of foul play on his body and, according to the police, no indications of forced entry into his apartment prior to his demise.

In summary, the autopsy or post-mortem examination concluded that Mr. Craig Boyd died from accidental prescription drug and alcohol abuse."

While Dr. Fuqua was rounding up his statement, Craig's father tried to suppress his sobs while Holly was visibly in tears. Breaking the silence that followed, the Coroner asked two clarifying questions about the quantity of drugs detected during the autopsy, as well as an estimate of the time of death. Once the records had been updated and no additional questions were forthcoming, the Coroner called for a short recess.

As the inquest drew to a close, the two legal representatives readied themselves to add their perspectives to the public record, based on what had transpired. Given the honour of making the final presentation was Redstone's lawyer, Leslie Howe, who did not pull any punches about why he was present at the inquest:

"Sir, I thank you for this opportunity to speak on behalf of Redstone Mortgage Plc.

First, permit me to extend the heartfelt condolences of the management and staff of Redstone to Mr. Craig Boyd's family. He was a talented and much-admired colleague who joined Redstone in 2002 as a graduate trainee, and quickly developed into one of our most prized and enterprising mortgage brokers.

The contagion of the financial crisis that began in the US in 2007-08 spread across the globe, not sparing the UK housing market. In the wake of the worst recession since the 1930s, a diverse group of casualties emerged.

One of those casualties was Redstone, a company that is currently fighting for its survival. Understandably, Redstone has had to downsize its workforce and to implement complementary strategies.

With this backdrop, we believe that the inclusion of Mr. Kelly's e-mail into the public domain will be prejudicial to Redstone's corporate interests and, frankly, damaging to its public image.

That concludes my submission.

Thank you."

In response, the Coroner said,

"Thank you, Mr. Howe, for your contributions to these proceedings. Your comments are duly noted.

If there are no other comments, I would like to end this phase of the inquest while I retire to consider the final verdict."

Below is the text of Her Majesty's Coroner for Brighton & Hove's findings of fact/conclusion in the inquest that preceded the registration of the death of Craig Boyd:

Surname: **Boyd**

Forename(s):   **Craig Henry**

Date/Place of
Birth: **6th June 1978**
                          Austin, Texas, USA

Date/Place of
Death: **28th March 2018**
                          4 Montpelier Road,
                          Brighton, BN1 3BB

Marital Status: **Single**

Occupation: **Mortgage Broker**

National
Insurance No.:   **XY5364757Z**

Date/Place

of Inquest: *16th August 2011*
                     Lewes Road, Brighton

Cause of death: *Alcohol/Drug-Related*

CHAPTER 7

Six months after the retrenchment and cost-cutting exercise at Redstone, the siege mentality at the company had intensified. Particularly among senior management, the sense of paranoia was relentless because many were struggling to hang on to their jobs. And ominously, the company was yet to return to profitability even as the stock price remained under severe pressure.

In such an atmosphere, the fallout from the Boyd inquest was like a red flag in the line of sight of a raging bull. Leslie Howe's feedback was received with collective angst and indignation. With cool heads in short supply, and the spooked bull stumbling into a china shop, the urge to lash out at Matt Kelly for his 'betrayal' left many foaming at the mouth. Paul Slade's visceral reaction was to hit back at anyone or anything that threatened the existence of Redstone. This left his colleagues in no doubt that Matt Kelly had crossed a red line into enemy territory.

Within days after the inquest verdict was published, Redstone's legal team drafted an action plan that was presented at the executive management meeting on Tuesday, 23rd August 2011. The underlying logic of the plan that was endorsed at that meeting was to show that Redstone was on the front foot, rather than on the defensive, and would not be pushed around.

First, the employment contract of Matt Kelly would be terminated. Second, Redstone would withdraw the preferential loan terms normally extended to all Redstone employees. In essence, Matt Kelly's outstanding mortgage and personal loans would immediately attract commercial interest rates, and compressed repayment durations. Putting such a financial squeeze on Matt appeared vindictive, and perhaps petty, but no one at the meeting raised any objection.

Third, a civil action would be filed at the High Court for a breach of confidence against Matt, following his decision to share privileged communication with a third party.

The following Thursday, Matt was invited to Redstone's corporate office in London for a meeting with a legal department executive, Phoebe Roe, and a senior HR Manager, Jane Stafford. Clueless about why he was being summoned, Matt turned up alone. Had he known what was on the agenda, he might have shown up with Roger Kincaid or one of his firm's solicitors. In anticipation of any blowback from the inquest, Mr. Boyd had, before returning to the US, told Matt that he could contact Mr. Kincaid's firm, if necessary.

Conducted in a focus room, the meeting kicked off at 11:00 a.m. Ms. Roe explained the purpose of the meeting, after which she handed Matt an official letter which read as follows:

"28 August 2011

Dear Mr. Kelly,

This letter is to inform you that your employment with Redstone Mortgage Plc is being terminated as of 12:00 noon today, 28 August 2011.

Following a review of our restructuring plans, the company has decided that your job is now surplus to requirements.

From the foregoing, please be informed that necessary adjustments to your existing mortgage and personal loans will be formally communicated to you by the Finance & Accounts department. Furthermore, arrangements will be made for you to receive all your outstanding wages, unpaid leave, and other entitlements, on the basis of your employment contract.

Please contact your People Manager in Brighton regarding the return of any company property in your possession.

On behalf of the management of Redstone, we thank you for your years of service and would like to extend our best wishes in all your future endeavours.

Sincerely,

HR Director
Redstone Mortgage Plc"

Matt re-read the letter, and then took a deep breath before responding,

"Honestly, I can't say that I'm surprised but did I have to come all the way to London for this meeting? Couldn't this have been handled in Brighton?"

Sounding more like a rhetorical statement than a question, Ms. Roe chose not to respond. Her colleague also remained silent. Sensing that the meeting was over, Matt thanked them and was soon on his way back to Brighton.

As Matt left London, Ms. Stafford examined her feelings about Redstone's treatment of Matt and his late friend, Craig, both of whom she remembered from their 2002 onboarding. In short, she was taken aback by the brutal manner of Matt's sacking. Based on her knowledge of the role that Matt played at Craig's inquest, it was obvious that Redstone was sending an overt message to potential whistle-blowers. But she was further shocked by Ms. Roe's vicious personal attack on Matt after his departure.

When Ms. Roe unveiled the outline of Redstone's civil claim against Matt, she was momentarily stunned into silence. Immediately, she knew she would raise the issue with her husband, Mr. Justice Jonathan Stafford. Without being naïve, she knew Redstone was exhibiting the characteristics of a cornered predator, but to turn on its own employees in such a vicious manner made her extremely uncomfortable.

That evening, just as Jane Stafford and her husband were settling down after dinner, Matt was on the phone to Skip Boyd. The six-hour time difference meant that Skip was up and about in his office in downtown Austin. Leaping up from his seat, his voice boomed down the phone line. Incensed beyond words, he asked Matt to read his dismissal letter back to him. Later, he requested for a copy to be scanned and e-mailed to him. At the end of their conservation, he told Matt to expect a call from Roger Kincaid.

As pragmatic as ever, Matt was not entirely surprised by the turn of events. The reality was that he was now well and truly out of a job and, having been on half pay for several months, his savings were beginning to dry up. Having been fired by Redstone, he knew that securing new employment could prove tricky in the prevailing job market. But of immediate concern was how to manage the outstanding loans on his car and the apartment. With his inside knowledge of how the property market operated, instantly he decided to cut costs by discontinuing his mortgage payments. And, before the wolves at Redstone barged down his front door, he would quickly apply for rental social housing through Brighton Homes.

Though his financial outlook was decidedly gloomy, Matt could not have envisioned the legal turbulence lurking around the corner. In the coming months, he was about to be hit by centrifugal legal forces that would bury him under an avalanche of lawsuits, far more than most people could expect in an entire lifetime.

CHAPTER 8

Fortuitously, the beginning of Matt Kelly's *annus horribilis* coincided with the creation of Her Majesty's Courts and Tribunals Service (HMCTS) as an agency of the Ministry of Justice. On 1st April 2011, the streamlining of court administration in England and Wales was conducted to achieve several objectives. Among these were to ensure that court cases were dealt with justly and at proportionate cost, with the goal of providing equal justice for all.

The HMCTS now aimed to use technology in creative ways and to handle lawsuits without the parties necessarily having to show up in court. Crucially, parties in dispute were encouraged to settle out of court when possible, since whoever lost typically had to pay the other party's legal costs. The new CPR (Civil Procedure Rules) for civil cases was therefore designed to make access to justice cheaper and faster, and within reach at the level of County and Crown Courts. Nevertheless, major disputes and the most important cases still wound their way to the High Court of Justice and Courts of Appeal, as deemed necessary. Falling in the latter category are disputes relating to business, commercial, intellectual property, breaches of trust and contract, and professional negligence.

In the event, the legal team at Redstone wasted no time in instituting the civil case *Redstone-v-Kelly* at the Chancery Division of the High Court of Justice in London. Situated at the *Rolls Building* along Fetter Lane, London, the incumbent Chancellor of the High Court had the responsibility of allocating hearings to 19 High Court Judges and 6 'Masters'.

In real life, only lazy or unimaginative script writers could be expected to generate frictionless plot lines, where coincidences save time and money in tightly-woven movie blockbusters. So, whether it was life imitating movies, or vice versa, the presiding Chancellor of the High Court randomly allocated *Redstone-v-Kelly* to, you guessed it, Mr. Justice Jonathan Stafford. Despite his thirty two-year legal experience, fifteen on the bench, Justice Stafford was momentarily dumbfounded when he browsed through the case file and recalled the discussion with his wife. How long ago was that?

Ever the professional, he buzzed his private secretary and dictated a short memo to the

Chancellor. In the interest of full disclosure, he disclosed that his wife worked at Redstone, and then added a brief summary of what she had told him about events preceding the *Redstone-v-Kelly* filing. In conclusion, he offered to recuse himself if that would better serve the course of justice.

Two days earlier, Phoebe Roe, by then playing the role of *Robin* to Leslie Howe's *Batman*, had supervised the completion in triplicate of Form N1 (*Claim Form (CPR Part 7)*). As approved by Redstone's management, the company was claiming the sum of £200,000 from the defendant, Matt Kelly, for sharing the content of a privileged document with a third party, in breach of his employment contract. Attached to the form was a £10,000 cheque, representing 5% of the claim amount. If eventually the case went to trial, Redstone would have to pay an additional £1,090. Instead of filing electronically, the documents were submitted the old-fashioned way – by hand – to the *Rolls Building*.

On receipt of Justice Stafford's memo, the Chancellor thanked him for his candour but insisted, in his written response, that he had full confidence in his ability and impartiality to hear the case. Thereafter, a sealed copy of the Claim Form, details of the claim contained in the *Particulars of Claim*, written evidence, along with a *Response Pack* (which included an *Acknowledgment of Service* form) were dispatched to Matt. He received the package on 12th September 2011, informing him that he was a defendant in the civil case *Redstone-v-Kelly*.

Boom!

Clearly, he did not see it coming. The court documents notified him that Redstone had instituted a 'breach of confidence' suit against him. Then, the realisation set in that Redstone was absolutely determined to ruin him, and to push him over the edge into bankruptcy.

£200,000! *B____ h__!!*

His next thought was that he was right to have stopped all future payments on his apartment. But that would appear to be the least of his immediate problems. After checking the time, he was immediately on the phone to Skip, who listened carefully before telling Matt that he would set up an appointment for him to see Mr. Kincaid the following day. He should go to the meeting with all the relevant documents because their strategy was now being elevated to a new level.

The following day, Matt arrived at Mr. Kincaid's office in London ten minutes early, but he was promptly ushered into his office. A jocular but deceptively sharp solicitor, Roger Kincaid was one half of the top-flight law firm *Major Kincaid*. Kincaid and his American friend and partner, Curtis Major, had qualified from law school the same year. While Kincaid focused on mainly civil cases, Major complemented him as one of London's most suave criminal defence lawyers.

Getting straight to the point, Kincaid handed Matt a two-page document, already signed off by Skip, which described their legal strategy. Kincaid told Matt that, at the end of the inquest, Skip had contemplated but later shelved the idea of initiating a civil lawsuit against Redstone. His hesitation was due to the fact that he had just invested in a new oil fracking project in the US which was eating up all his time. After brainstorming with Holly, Skip realised that she was not particularly interested in seeking justice on behalf of Craig, who she felt should be allowed to rest in peace. However, when Redstone went after Matt, Skip opted to hit back at them – hard.

To that end, Kincaid told Matt that his firm would be filing a suit against Redstone within a week, claiming damages and restitution in the amount of £1 million. The kernel of their civil case would be based on Redstone's lack of empathy, bordering on professional negligence, in the premature death of Craig Boyd. As part of their strategy, Skip suggested that Matt should also file for unfair dismissal at an Employment Tribunal, either in London or back in Brighton.

Matt then seized the moment to raise the issue of the mortgage loans that he and Craig had obtained from Redstone some years back. Matt said that he was aware that Major Kincaid was managing Craig's estate. As for him, he told Kincaid about his plan to default on his mortgage payments since he wanted to focus all his attention on the current lawsuits. When the dust finally settled, he could look for a new job and start afresh.

Kincaid thought that his plan made a lot of sense since, under the circumstances, Redstone was unlikely to cut him any slack but would probably evict him at the drop of a hat. Continuing, Kincaid told Matt that Skip was willing to support him financially in the coming months. He had also instructed him that, at the minimum, all of Matt's legal expenses should be routed through *Major Kincaid.*

Before the meeting concluded, Matt presented all the documents he had received from the High Court. Kincaid read through them quickly and then got Matt to sign all the relevant sections. He told Matt that they would reply within the stipulated 14 days, but would also request for more time to prepare a formal response. In the interim, *Major Kincaid* would serve all the necessary papers pertaining to *Boyd-v-Redstone* which, he reckoned, should keep Redstone busy for a while. For easier coordination, Kincaid thought it would be best if *Major Kincaid* instituted the unfair dismissal case at the Employment Tribunal in London, rather than Brighton.

Lastly, in order to avoid putting undue pressure on Matt, and to conserve money, lawyers from *Major Kincaid* would represent him at future court dates, except when his presence was absolutely essential.

Now, before lodging a claim at an Employment Tribunal, a claimant is usually advised to first contact ACAS (the Advisory, Conciliation and Arbitration Service) to explore opportunities for conciliation. However, Kincaid decided to bypass the ACAS route altogether. Therefore, in short order, all the necessary papers were filed for the case *Kelly-v-Redstone* at the Employment Tribunal located at 30-34 Kingsway, London.

And true to his word, Redstone received from the High Court of Justice in early October 2011, the Claim Form and other supporting documentation for *Boyd-v-Redstone*.

Confused?

Before *Major Kincaid* shut down for the 2011 Christmas holidays, the legal teams of both parties held a case management conference to agree a timetable for sharing evidence prior to a trial date of Tuesday, 6th March 2012. Duly approved by Justice Stafford, the decision was also taken to hear the lawsuits *Redstone-v-Kelly* (Redstone's original suit) and *Boyd-v-Redstone* concurrently. From all the parties' points of view, combining the suits made perfect sense since all the issues were unusually interwoven.

After three consecutive months of missed payments, a possession claim was lodged by Redstone at the Brighton County Court against Matt (to minimise crossed wires, the possession case would be dubbed *Redstone-v-Kelly II)*. And to ring in the New Year, Matt received the anticipated eviction notice from Redstone. But since he had already vacated the apartment and moved to a council flat in central Brighton, the letter did not reach him until the second week in January 2012.

As crazy as it might sound, Matt ensured that, throughout his months of travails, he kept his parents and fiancé out of the loop. Although, like everyone else, they were aware that the property market was in turmoil, Matt concluded that it would serve no useful purpose to burden them with his personal problems. Perhaps someday, when he was able to come up for air, he would regale them with a colourful account of how he was ostracised by Redstone, but remained unbowed.

CHAPTER 9

On 2nd February 2012, the Employment Tribunal in London sat to consider a slew of pending lawsuits. On the daily list was *Kelly-v-Redstone* which was scheduled to begin at 11:00 a.m. Presiding was a three-man panel led by an Employment Judge, minus wig and gown, and two lay members in a setting less formal than a courtroom. Nevertheless, all those giving evidence were expected to do so under oath.

Matt had arrived at the office of *Major Kincaid* by 9:00 a.m. that morning to go over their strategy for the tribunal. Present at the briefing with Kincaid and Matt was Janice Lohan, one of the firm's experts on employment law. Going in, she explained that their goal was not to get Matt reinstated to his old job nor to necessarily extract monetary compensation. Instead, she intended to spotlight the fact that Matt was fired without just cause. For Matt's benefit, Kincaid added that their plan was to utilise, through referral, the tribunal verdict at the more important hearing taking place later at the High Court. Matt's role would be to describe at the Employment Tribunal the basic outline of his participation at the Boyd inquest, and his subsequent dismissal by Redstone.

Representing Redstone at the tribunal was Phoebe Roe, accompanied by a junior associate. On the opposing side were Janice and Matt. From the evidence provided by Phoebe, she laid out the chronology of Matt's suspension to his final dismissal, careful to stick to the argument that the company's actions were driven solely by business considerations. After Matt had given his evidence, Janice followed up by asserting that Matt was dismissed without cause. She claimed that Redstone's action was based on the respondent's malicious reaction to the claimant's solicitation e-mail on behalf of his late colleague. She provided further context by notifying the tribunal about the pending 'breach of confidence' case filed against the claimant at the High Court.

When the tribunal judge sought a response from the respondent, Phoebe stuck to her earlier position and refused to accept that the dismissal was without cause. After additional probing from panel members, the final judgment was delivered just shy of 1:00 p.m.

In its ruling, the tribunal urged the two parties to explore the possibility of reaching a private settlement within 14 days. Failing this, the panel would take the unusual step of referring its findings through HMCTS to the High Court so that the case could be merged with *Redstone-v-Kelly*. Needless to say, the two-week deadline passed without the parties bothering to comply. And so, the unfair dismissal claim ended up on Justice Stafford's desk, thus making a complex case that much more complicated.

Meanwhile, at the Brighton County Court, Redstone wasted no time in enforcing its rights to take full possession of Matt's apartment. Having reneged on his payments, and failing to respond to Redstone's request to clear the arrears, *Redstone-v-Kelly II* was disposed of during a brief telephone hearing on 13th February 2012 between a District Judge and the lender's enforcement officer. However, since Matt had already vacated the premises and handed in the keys to the property, there was no need to send in bailiffs to effect eviction, as would normally have been the case.

With little else to do but wait for the big one, Matt had more than enough time on his hands to reflect on the past decade. Whatever the outcome of the High Court case, which was scheduled to run over two to three days, he knew that he would be able to look on his life in a bifurcated way – before and after 6th March 2012. Sadly, this was an option that was closed to Craig, a fact that made him angrier than ever. Without question, Redstone had defined his career so far, but there was no reason why he could not make a fresh start after the trial. Deep down, he knew that Redstone was not solely to blame for Craig's death. Rather, greed, poor financial control and wilful ignorance had helped to create a bubble that inevitably brought the industry to its knees. That said, it was important that companies, if not individuals, should be held accountable for their actions or, perhaps in the case of Redstone, inaction.

Matt was yet to decide on his next career move. However, he was certain that he wanted no further part in the housing or financial services industry. For years, he had nursed the idea of working for one of several non-governmental organisations or charities focused on climate change and the environment. So far in his life, that represented a road less travelled. But, at the moment, all tracks led directly to the *Rolls Building*.

CHAPTER 10

By protocol, civil cases in the High Court are normally heard by a single judge. Judge Jonathan Stafford was well aware of the challenge of preparing for the amalgamated 'Redstone-Kelly-Boyd' case, which did not require a jury. Expectedly, judges would normally review and draw upon previous High Court decisions although, as the third highest court in the land, High Court judges are bound by the doctrine of precedent. In other words, their rulings must align with existing decisions of the Court of Appeal, the Supreme Court and the Court of Justice of the European Union.

Parties in High Courts, especially those with deep pockets, could always be expected to appeal an unfavourable verdict. To that extent, judges strive to adhere closely to the letter of the law, and precedents. Despite the assistance provided by paralegals and other support staff, in reality this was easier said and done. Without being facetious, occasionally it required the proverbial wisdom of King Solomon to untangle multi-faceted cases such as 'Redstone-Kelly-Boyd.'

Privately-educated Jonathan Stafford had been both a keen cricketer and a Boy Scout. Though baptised in the Church of England, his sense of fairness and social justice was anchored more on his brief flirtation with Marxism than his religious beliefs. After graduating from Durham University, and later called to the Bar, his ideological leanings had gradually shifted from leftist to right-of-centre. True to his background, Justice Stafford was a straight arrow whose allegiance to his oath of office was near-impeccable.

Following the initial discussion with his wife, Jane, about the pending case, his last reference to it at home was to inform her about the decision of the Chancellor of the High Court to entrust him with the hearing. As the date of the trial drew nearer, he stayed up later than usual, and she knew better than to disturb his concentration.

Ahead of the hearing, the two gunslingers – Leslie Howe and Roger Kincaid – had been fencing and jousting furiously, all in an effort to gain some psychological advantage. And although witness statements and ancillary documentation had been filed, both sides chose to have their key witnesses take the stand. This meant that Paul Slade, the chief executive of Redstone, Skip Boyd, Matt Kelly and a

Coroner's Officer, representing Brighton's Chief Coroner, were all scheduled to appear in court.

Among this cast of characters, Paul Slade was easily the most fascinating. Born Paul Benedict Solowitz and brought up by a single mother, he changed his surname to Slade at age nineteen soon after completing his A-levels. Unable to afford a university education, but a math whiz who recorded 'A' grades in Mathematics and Business Studies and a 'C' in Government, Paul started out as an apprentice stockbroker. Within five years, while working alongside more experienced staff, he acquired levels 4 through 7 qualifications – equivalent to a Bachelor's degree. With unerring focus, Paul became a chartered stockbroker by age 26, after passing two Bank of England-sanctioned professional examinations. Afterwards, he was seconded to an investment company in New York for nine months. And it was on that trip that he began to hatch his entrepreneurial dreams.

Although not a Tory by birth, Paul was a big fan of Margaret Thatcher, whose privatisation and free market policies seemed like a godsend for an ambitious young man. Teaming up with two like-minded colleagues, Redstone began life just before Thatcher was ousted from power in late 1990.

Through clever financial engineering and a series of mergers and acquisitions transactions, Redstone grew into a recognisable powerhouse in the UK housing market. As time passed, Paul Slade never married and went on to channel all his creativity and energy into Redstone.

Street-smart and hungry for material success, Paul understood the psychology of the class-conscious British society. Never a stranger to clichés, he recognised that, without the right family and school connections, he needed to compensate with other skill sets. To blend into high society, he paid special attention to his wardrobe and grooming, and took elocution lessons to improve his communication skills. Despite these efforts, this carefully cultivated mask occasionally slipped to expose the real Paul Slade, usually when he became rattled or when under enormous pressure.

Three weeks before Paul Slade's planned appearance at the High Court on 6th March, Redstone received a letter that the company had been dreading for months. Due to its precarious situation, the Financial Services Authority (FSA) of the Bank of England invited Redstone to a meeting on Monday, 12th March 2012 to discuss its future prospects. Slated so soon after the court trial, the

FSA summons set off Paul Slade and the leadership of Redstone, who had begun to view the trial as an irritant they wished would simply disappear.

On a personal level, the implication of the face-to-face meeting with the FSA unearthed some of Paul's hidden insecurities. Regardless of how successful he had become, he always felt that the sneering stuffy suits at the Bank of England viewed him as just another grasping 'barrow boy' who was out of his depth. Furthermore, despite the fact that he owned two multi-million pound properties in London, he never forgot his upbringing in a council flat in an East End tower block. Therefore, it could be deduced that, psychologically, Paul was not in the best frame of mind in early March 2012.

Prior to the trial, Justice Stafford had decided that he would hear Redstone's evidence to the two lawsuits *Redstone-v-Kelly* and *Boyd-v-Redstone*, as the claimant and then the defendant, respectively. Evidently, it was clear that central to the two cases were Redstone's response to Craig Boyd's health problems, Matt Kelly's e-mail alert, and the fallout from the Boyd inquest. Much was therefore riding on Paul Slade's testimony, as the corporate leader whose company's policies were at the intersection of the cases, including the unfair dismissal suit filed on behalf of Matt Kelly.

After the discovery phase, the parties had the opportunity to settle each of the cases out of court, or to go to arbitration. As anticipated, none of Howe or Kincaid or their clients was interested in exploring this option, and so the trial beckoned.

On the appointed date, the weather outside the High Court was cool but the relationship between the opposing parties was even chillier. After everyone was seated in Court Room 7, the court clerk asked them to rise as Justice Stafford strode in.

When he was invited to deliver his opening statement, Leslie Howe began by describing the genesis of Redstone Mortgage Plc. He spoke about the company's humble beginnings to becoming a FTSE darling in less than two decades. He mentioned the entrepreneurial spirit that fostered Redstone's rapid growth, and its contributions to the UK economy, in terms of mortgage lending, job creation and philanthropy. To record such achievements, Howe claimed that Redstone hired exceptional individuals who were strong mentally and physically, and who enabled Redstone to excel in a highly competitive market.

When he finally addressed Redstone's claim against Matt Kelly and its defence in *Boyd-v-Redstone*, Howe reminded the court about the US sub-prime housing crisis and the ensuing global recession. He contended that Redstone was facing an existential threat, like several other companies, starting in late 2008. He also acknowledged the stresses and difficulties at Redstone impinged on management, employees, customers and other stakeholders.

Looking directly at Skip Boyd, he expressed Redstone's shock and anguish following the death of his son, Craig. Rather dramatically, he paused for well over a minute with his head bowed before continuing. Thereafter, he reiterated Redstone's contention that as an employee, Matt Kelly breached his employer's confidence by divulging internal privileged information to a third party. In essence, that was the crux of the civil case before the High Court.

In his reply, Kincaid cleverly latched on to Howe's final statement. However, he based his side's argument on what he described as Redstone's toxic corporate culture. In his opinion, Redstone was a secretive and negligent employer that cared more about the bottom line than the welfare of its workforce. He conceded that Redstone had been a positive force for the UK economy. Nevertheless, that fact could not shield its leadership from the consequences of its poor judgment, including the company's defective business practices.

The stage was now set for the cross-examination phase of the trial and, unsurprisingly, the most penetrating and impactful evidence was provided by Paul Slade, as described in this abridged portrayal:

"Please state your name for the record," began Roger Kincaid.

"Paul Slade."

"You are a co-founder and the current chief executive of Redstone Mortgage Plc, is that correct?"

"Correct."

"Can you please confirm that, as the chief executive of Redstone Mortgage Plc, you are the claimant in the High Court Case Number

RK89JH2, and the defendant in Case Number BR007YU?"

"*Yes, I am.*"

"*Is it a fact that Craig Boyd was employed by Redstone on 2nd September 2002?*"

"*He was.*"

"*Would you accept that, leading up to the 2008 housing market crisis, Redstone relaxed its underwriting policy and internal controls to accommodate sub-prime borrowers?*"

"*Our policy was market-driven.*"

"*Is that a yes or no?*"

"*Yes.*"

"*Would you agree that Redstone was overly aggressive in seeking greater market share?*"

Rising to address Justice Stafford, Howe interjected,

"*Your Honour, is this question relevant to the hearing?*"

"*I will allow it. To move this along, Mr. Howe, henceforth, I will decide what is relevant or not. The witness should please answer the question.*"

"*Redstone did what was necessary to compete effectively, and to enhance shareholder value,*" replied Paul.

"***OK. Broadly, over the years, how would you characterise the job performance of Craig Boyd?***"

"*Craig Boyd was a valued member of his team at Brighton. According to his personnel records, he was rated consistently above average.*"

"***In the aftermath of the property crisis, who did your staff consult when under pressure from aggrieved borrowers?***"

"*Line managers and HR professionals.*"

"***Very briefly, can you describe the nature of Redstone's employee wellness programme?***"

"*Redstone does not have an internal wellness programme. We expect our employees to utilise the services of the National Health Service.*"

*"**Would you accept that Redstone's provision for its employees' mental health is inadequate?**"*

Upset by the implied insinuation, Paul blurted out,

"I challenge the premise of that question. When contacted, our HR department is equipped to make the appropriate referrals for employees with mental health issues."

*"**In that case, is it not true that after you received an e-mail dated 8th February 2011 (Exhibit 4), from Mr. Kelly, and in a most insensitive manner, Redstone placed Mr. Boyd on administrative leave?**"*

"The two events were completely unconnected."

*"**Would you please answer yes or no?**"*

Even though Leslie Howe had warned him to expect that line of questioning, Paul appeared indignant. Strident and visibly tetchy, he replied,

"Look here, I have a business to run... Redstone is not a charity organisation, but a public

company that is answerable to investors and shareholders. Last time I checked, our compensation packages are among the most generous in our industry."

"**Be that as it may, can I submit that a culture of omnipotence, triumphalism and denial existed at Redstone prior to the credit crisis?**"

"*I absolutely disagree.*"

"**In that case, was it the sense of vulnerability and the dread of bad publicity – caused by the release of a copy of Matt Kelly's e-mail at the inquest into Mr. Boyd's death – that spurred Mr. Kelly's dismissal?**"

Incandescent, Leslie Howe was quickly on his feet,

"*Your Honour, Your Honour…*"

"*Enough! I would like to see Mr. Howe and Mr. Kincaid in my chambers. Right now!*" declared Justice Stafford.

When the hearing resumed, the judge steered Paul's cross-examination and re-examination to a conclusion, but not before asking a few clarifying questions of his own. At 4:45 p.m., he adjourned the hearing to the following day.

Overnight, Howe and Kincaid worked hard at polishing their closing statements which would provide the final opportunity to sway the judge's ruling. To the neutral observer, it appeared that Kincaid had succeeded in reframing the multi-pronged case, and focusing much attention on the leadership of Paul Slade and his company's internal culture.

To add more pressure on Redstone, Skip Boyd's emotional turn on the stand transmitted very powerfully a father's unbearable grief at the loss of his son. Prior to the crisis, Skip claimed that Craig loved his job, and saw nothing but blue sky in his future. Skip was convinced that his son's drinking problem was triggered by the stress at work, and the family was unaware that he was abusing prescription drugs.

Predictably, the closing arguments leant close to each side's interpretation of the stack of evidence. In the end, it fell on Justice Stafford to deliver his verdict.

Well, not so fast.

EPILOGUE

By late spring 2018, the author could not escape newspaper headlines that reminded readers that the tenth anniversary of the Lehman Brothers debacle was only months away. Quite rightly, columnists and opinion page writers were asking what exactly had changed since the autumn of 2008.

According to David Kynaston, the author of *Till Time's Last Stand*, a book about the history of the Bank of England, he surmised that financial crises tend to occur approximately every 10 years. With that knowledge, it would be logical to expect policy makers to consciously implement palliatives designed to prevent history repeating itself. If only it were that simple, or that easy to tame the animal spirits that undergird the capitalist system. Another keen observation attributed to Mr. Kynaston was that, over the past 200 years, financial crises tended to originate in the US. However, several analysts have suggested that the next financial crisis could very well start in China, now the world's second largest economy.

In an ever more interconnected and globalised world predicated on fostering winners and losers, one could do worse than to revisit the folksy wisdom of Warren Buffett. Also known as the *Sage of Omaha* (as in Omaha, small town, USA), Mr. Buffett once declared that *"Only when the tide goes out do you discover who's been swimming naked."* In other words, it is impossible to legislate against excessive risk-taking, greed and stupidity, especially when it comes to man and *Mammon*.

Another inconvenient truth postulates that any contagion in one location very quickly spreads to other parts. Indications are that, in the UK for instance, property prices in 2018 are once again booming and consumer debts remain excessively high. With interest rates still relatively low, at 0.25%, could this be a recipe for another credit bubble? Others have predicted that the next crisis could begin with the collapse of the bitcoin cyber-currency. Controversially, incumbent US President Donald Trump's imposition of unilateral tariffs could ignite a dangerous tit-for-tat trade war that could easily escalate, and drag the global economy back to the nightmare of the 1930s.

As far as Matt Kelly was concerned, beginning in 2013, his life had moved in a radically different direction. No longer a subscriber to the *Financial Times* and *Property Week*, he listened to his gut by establishing a nascent environmental publication called *Now or Never*. His editorial advocacy suggested a closing window of opportunity to reverse past failed policies on the environment. Starting with a blog, he later added a print edition after securing advertising deals from two renewable energy companies. With two full-time researchers and seven part-time, multinational digital assistants, *Now or Never* expanded to include French and German editions, with a Mandarin version in the pipeline.

Looking in his rear-view mirror, he was pleased that he had finally put Redstone behind him.

When Justice Stafford's ruling was delivered, Matt was not in court. According to Roger Kincaid, the approved judgment ran to over 100 pages, almost as lengthy as this book, if you can believe it. In its standard format, it contained legalistic prose structured under: (1) Introduction; (2) The issues; (3) Factual background; (4) The evidence; (5) The arguments advanced by the parties; and so on. Mercifully, a summarised four-page version was e-mailed to Matt. The header contained the caveat that the summary did not spell out all the reasons for the final decision; that is, the full judgment of the Court was the only authoritative document.

Taking into account all the competing positions, and after reviewing precedent judgments and approaches to the quantification of damages in similar claims, Justice Stafford ruled as follows:

1. Redstone Mortgage Plc erred in law by insisting that Matt Kelly's e-mail message dated 8th February 2011, and later presented at the inquest into the death of Craig Boyd, contravened its confidentiality policy.

2. The presentation of the e-mail message at the inquest by Mr. Kelly was not an unconscionable act, but rather a public-spirited reaction to a tragic incident.

3. The stressful work environment at Redstone Mortgage Plc was principally responsible for the decline in Craig Boyd's mental health.

4. Despite the financial distress plaguing Redstone Mortgage Plc, the company could have done more to support Craig Boyd and other employees under duress.

5. Based on the evidence presented, the Court would give Redstone Mortgage Plc the benefit of the doubt about the reasons adduced for terminating Matt Kelly's employment. At the time, it was noted that as many as a third of the workforce was retrenched.

6. In conclusion, the Court hereby orders Redstone Mortgage Plc to pay the following damages:

- *£720,000 to the estate of Mr. Craig Boyd*

- *£90,000 to Mr. Matt Kelly*

- *However, all parties shall be liable for their respective legal costs*

7. Redstone Mortgage Plc has the legal right to appeal this judgment within the next 28 days.

Without much hesitation, and within the next seventy-two hours, Leslie Howe submitted Redstone's application at the Court of Appeal, thereby effectively challenging Justice Stafford's verdict. Before he travelled back to the US, Skip Boyd invited Matt to dinner to celebrate the end of the trial. He insisted that he was not particularly exercised by the financial compensation. Rather, justice was being served and he hoped that other companies would learn the right lessons from Redstone's lapses. Both Skip and Matt were aware that the appeal process could be protracted, but they were more than reassured about the quality of *Major Kincaid's* legal representation.

Out of the blue, the news reached Skip and Matt about four months following the High Court hearing that the FSA had sanctioned and approved the acquisition of Redstone by DLT Building Society. Some sections of the media tried to spin the event as a merger between equals, but industry insiders knew better. By then, Redstone remained exposed to sub-prime and commercial loans, as the quality of its asset portfolio continued to erode. Those axed, as part of the negotiated deal, included almost three-quarters of the top management cadre of Redstone. While many senior executives retained their shareholding in the merged entity, there simply was no room for them in the new management structure.

Predictably, the most devastated of all was Paul Slade who felt that his entire life's work had gone down the drain. It might be objectionable to compare his experience with a marital divorce or the loss of a child, but only Paul could truly describe how numb he felt. For the first time since his childhood, he went into a rabbit hole of introspection. And although he seemed to be financially secure, he was left adrift without any visible anchor. Still, one thing was certain: there was no way that Paul would hit the bottle. He was a health freak, and too canny to fall into that trap. But as a marathoner, maybe he would hit the road and keep running, and running, in the pursuit of a more judicious heart.

Meanwhile, the reconstituted Board of DLT Building Society instructed its legal advisers to review all outstanding lawsuits in the enlarged group. Having followed the *Boyd-Redstone* case in the press, and the negative publicity associated with it, the signal from the new management was that it wanted the lawsuit settled out of court. To that end, contact with *Major Kincaid* led to negotiations and a quick resolution. Sealed with a *Tomlin Order*, the agreement was signed by both parties, approved by Justice Stafford, and duly resolved at the High Court.

The court resolution showed that DLT agreed to a 20% reduction in Justice Stafford's judgment orders. Skip insisted on covering all the legal fees due to *Major Kincaid*, thus leaving Matt with a healthy bank balance. Soon afterwards, *Now or Never* came into existence in Matt's living-room. Knowing that the publication needed to grow into a self-sustaining entity, Matt tapped into his business background to design a revenue model based on advertisement and subscription fees.

Skip and Holly later established the *Craig Boyd Foundation* in the UK to provide private support to young people with mental health issues. Matt was invited to join the foundation's Board of Trustees, which was chaired by Roger Kincaid.

Looking forward, Matt was gratified that the foundation would serve as a memorial platform for Craig, but he also knew that nothing could bring back his old friend. Indeed, there was no guarantee that he would have better luck in his quest to save our blue-tinged planet, but it was a safe, if morbid, bet that he would die trying.

www.ingramcontent.com/pod-product-compliance
Lightning Source LLC
Chambersburg PA
CBHW071325220526
45468CB00001B/502